Delicat

Delicate Whispers

By Ahmed Bashir

Cover design by Andy Kwok and Ahmed Bashir

Drawings courtesy of Jabbar Bashir

For Khaye

Her heart a fallen star

Its purity from this world afar

Authors note

Love is an amazing natural intoxicant that affects people in many different ways. One only need look at history. The Pharaoh Ramses II built an amazing temple for Nefretari, whom he referred to as "the one for whom the sun shines".

Shah Jahan many years later built the Taj Mahal for his loved one, whom he referred to as the "jewel of the palace". On her death, he was so heartbroken, it is rumoured that he ordered the court into mourning for two years, and he was never the same again.

Closer to home, my Grandfather didn't build a Taj Mahal or a temple but was deeply affected by the loss of my grandmother. The difference in him was palpable; all his energy and sparkle had departed his frail frame with the passing of my grandmother. Grandfather would often tell me how he lost his mother when he was very young. He would explain how "A boy is not lost or broken on the loss of his mother and the severing of the bond between mother and child, but a man is forever lost and broken on the loss of the one that is most special and loved, one's soul mate."

In my own encounter with love, I learned that love is about the entwining of souls, the sharing of a breath, and that the words "I love you" are not nearly enough to convey the depth of connection one has with the one they love. I find poetry a powerful medium to communicate the intensity and complexity of the emotions of which the heart in love is overflowing.

This collection of poems is a personal exploration of the inspirational and fearsome journey of my own heart through love, based on real events, dreams, and musings. Opening the collection is a short story which introduces the dynamic symphony of joy and tragedy that encompasses the two lovers, whose journey – together and apart – is the subject of this work. The poems, however, do not depict a chronological narrative, but are divided into two main parts: cheerful and tearful! And a few, such as "I told her," are just for fun.

Contents

The Whistling Trees **13**

Cheerful Whispers **23**

Journeys end 25

Be with it 28

Tomorrow 29

It is me 31

Sailor 32

I told her 34

My one and only 35

A short love letter 36

Lost 39

You are 40

Oh how 41

The beast 43

Love sick 44

Amazing 46

Do 47

Khaye 48

The one 50

Proposal 51

Never forgotten 53

Our park 54

Cognitive lapse 55

In the shade of the coconut tree 57

A full moon tonight 59

Intoxicated Dreamer 60

I can see 62

We 65

My flower lady 66

Precious gift 69

For as long 71

Wedding vow 73

Day away 74

Without a word 77

No more sharing 79

My sweet maid 80

For only thee 82

My secret 83

Echo 85

Tearful Whispers 87

Lovers parted 89

The last goodbye 91

Beside my love 92

Cuffed 95

Awaiting the day 97

Never alone 98

One midsummer's day 100

Why does it feel so real? 102

Awaiting thee 103

On my way 104

Why not me? 106

Foreseen 108

Prettiest Pear 111

A little wiser....112
The bed....113
Immortal is me....114
Cut from the rose....116
Fear mere me....119
The calling....121
Left behind....122
Fair swap....123
Prayer....124
Gone....125
Elephant driver....126
Beloved's road....128
Listen....129
Melancholy....130
One more whisper....131

The Whistling Trees

Crammed into a Ford Focus, my friends and I left Granada in the late afternoon, and travelled for hours, before driving down a dirt track, which led into darkness. We passed the jagged remains of what looked like an old stone house, maybe it was from Spain's Moorish past, the car headlights revealing a dilapidated structure filled with gaping holes, as if shelled by a tank. We had all sorts of conversations during the journey, one in particular becoming slightly heated – about poverty and corruption in Pakistan, and how the Taliban, scourging through the country like some obscene infection, had plunged an already grim situation into chaotic devastation. But my mind was elsewhere. I didn't say much, pretending I was tired; closing my eyes in the back-seat and withdrawing into my own world.

Beneath my eyelids, I watched her smiling and playing with her vast curly hair, a bird's nest is what she would call it, but I liked it.

"Sorry where? I didn't hear you properly," I said. She paused knowing that I'd heard exactly what she'd said.

"Paa-kiss-tan" she repeated again as she described a time when she was very young and had travelled to Pakistan with her parents. I loved her voice and pronunciation of the word "Pakistan" and I would try to get her to say it again and again. She said it with an American accent she'd picked up whilst out there for a few years studying.

She told me how whilst in Pakistan she would sneak off against her parent's wishes, off across the road, to an elderly gentleman with a spicy chickpea stand in the street. She loved the chickpeas, but enjoyed helping sell them even more, telling people how nice they were. She attracted a lot of attention from the passers-by, so the stand owner liked having her around. It was good for business; she stood out with her thick curly blond hair and pale white complexion. She told me how she had acquired the best chickpea recipe, could make the most splendid chickpeas and would make some someday especially for me; I had thought the day would be soon. It never crossed my mind that this day would never come.

The car braked abruptly. I quickly dried my eyes and wiped my cheeks before somebody noticed. Apparently, we were lost. The guys decided we should all get out of the car and search for light coming from any nearby buildings.

The night was cold, beautiful and clear, shimmering with stars, and the moon full and incredibly bright. Small creatures shuffled through the shrubbery. I walked down the dirt track away from the light of the headlights and towards the intense blackness, looking up at the stars, as the wind whistled softly, playing in the trees.

Khaye always kept her windows open, whether it was warm or cold. Like me, she loved the peaceful sound of the wind in the trees. We spent countless nights in the backdrop of this mysteriously splendid sound, chatting about anything and everything. Once we joked together about how many children we would have and what we would name them. "I want 9, yes 9" she teased, and I laughingly agreed.

She asked me what name I'd like if we'd have a boy.

"Alam," I responded. Khaye liked this name too as it was similar to her father's name.

"What name would you like for a girl," I asked.

Without hesitation she replied, "Elisa." I instantly liked it. So we were agreed: Alam and Elisa.

"Lets go", came a loud voice from behind me. "I just spoke to Shahnaz and she's meeting us at the Puebla," shouted Shiraz as he walked past a headlight, casting a momentary shadow in front of the car. We needed someone to guide us. Having phoned the hosts to apologise for being so late we were told to head back down the main road to the Puebla de don Fedrique from where a member of staff would show us the way.

I sauntered back to the car, taking the time to again clear my watery eyes, coughing through the lump in my throat and blowing my nose. Only the darkness prevented my friends from seeing the state I was in. Whilst walking back I was startled by the hoot of an owl. I suddenly felt inspired. I pulled my phone out of my pocket and with the aid of the screen LED typed some lines into my phone:

"O it's a full moon tonight, how the wise one is in full flight, as the fairies gather for a fight, a shooting star does create a pretty sight".

Khaye loves books and poetry, a passion we share. I would try and impress her with my own, which had begun flowing like never before early in our relationship, but more so since she told me about her illness, the first time a tsunami had hit my heart.

Back in the car, we played some old Indian music off a CD. The song was one of Khaye's favourites. Sometimes she would ring me and if there was no answer leave a recording of a song. The song was always a surprise and I loved her doing that. We would also send each other photos of trees, flowers, and architecture, every time something amazing caught our eyes. We appreciated the beauty around us and Khaye had even singlehandedly created her own stunning garden, full of exotic plants and scents.

"Arggh... I could kill that Peanut" she would say every time she planted flowers, Peanut, the resident squirrel, would always dig them up.

The car stopped on arrival at the Puebla and we parked up near a small fountain. It was now pitch black outside, but my eyes were drawn to shafts of light from a pair of windows across from our ad hoc parking spot. Through them I spotted an old couple. The woman seemed to be mopping the floor as I watched, then I realised the lady had stopped, and was standing still, staring at me quizzically. She must have wondered who we were and what on earth we were doing out there in the early hours of the morning. She gazed at me and the others, as we gazed back at her, even while she disappeared from one window and reappeared at another, mopping away. I admired the couple as I thought about the dreams I'd had of growing old with Khaye. I'd seen us old and wrinkly, working in the garden together, lovingly competing and arguing about who had grown the best strawberries and corn. I'd never expected my dreams to be shattered.

"My operation is in a few days and I don't want you to visit me," she said and she always meant what she said, so I obliged her, although I so wanted to be by her side. Whilst she was in hospital, we would spend all night speaking to each other on the phone. We'd even speak or text during the day when the nurses weren't about. Her voice became more and more upbeat as time passed, and we both hoped and believed that the cancer had been caught early, and that soon everything would be fine.

"BEEP BEEP" went the horn of our guide who'd finally arrived. We followed her jeep to the foothills of the La Sagra. When we finally got out of our car I wished we hadn't. It was so cold, my teeth chattered violently. We decided we all needed a hot mug of tea, although I was less keen than the others. With hands outstretched and taking each step hesitantly in the darkness, we followed each other, stepping tentatively through a small courtyard with a small fountain in the centre. By the time we arrived at the main building of the complex, I was grumbling to myself, do we really need this tea, I could just do with a shower and some sleep. But Khaye loves a cup of tea before bed and would have encouraged me to have one. I noticed the log-fire in the corner of the room and stared at its beautiful colours, my mind drifting whilst the heat of the tea enlivened my frozen lips.

It was while at work enjoying a nice, hot cup of green tea, that a second tsunami hit my heart. I'd known something wasn't right. Khaye had been quiet for a few days and I could hear in her voice that she was upset and had been crying. She finally told me that the results were grim, that it had spread. My heart was pounding to fever pitch, my mind in a frenzy, I hurled my paper-work across my desk and grabbed my bag rushing out the office. I headed straight for Euston and got on a train.

If you love me please don't come," were her words just as the train took off.

I tried to convince her but as always to no avail. I arrived in Birmingham and got off the train. I stretched my legs, already drenched in the pouring rain, and then got back on again without seeing her. Tears drenched my face the length of the return journey, as I pencilled a poem in my notebook.

The crackling of the open fire woke me from my reminiscing. I finished my tea and headed to the sleeping quarters. I couldn't sleep and lay in bed, wondering how she was feeling. Had she eaten? I knew how horrendous the chemo was, how it forced her to lose her appetite and feel awful.

In the silence I heard her lilting voice and sweet laugh. I wished, futilely, that I'd receive a text from her, telling me she was thinking of me and wondering whether I'd arrived in Spain ok. She loved Spain, it was one of her most favourite places. She loved the history of the Moors, and had a large collection of books on the subject. I lay there thinking about how she was so passionate about so many things; how she loved helping people, from the young to the elderly; how she taught blind children music every weekend and was so concerned about their development. I thought, why God? Why her? As sleep slowly dragged me away, the words echoed round my skull: A most gentle and kind being, why her, why her?

I had a beautiful dream that night. I was with her and we were lying in bed together. Between us was a bed sheet which covered my face. Through the sheet I had my arms around her, squeezing her against me.

She was talking to me and then suddenly pulled the duvet from my face and said "Are you even listening?"

I moved forward and kissed her. "Of course I am sweetheart."

We sat up, our eyes fixed to each other as we kissed again. Then my eyes caught the clock: it was 10:30. Oh dear, I was ridiculously late for work. But I didn't want to leave. I just wanted to stay with her and told her so.

"I'm going to phone in sick, and spend the day with you," I said as I grabbed the phone. Before dialling, I began practicing a sick voice as she teased me and smiled. Her smile was so amazingly beautiful; it felt like time had stood still. I dialled and the phone began to ring. She put her arms around me and squeezed me against her. Then as the phone was answered, I was awake.

Someone was snoring from the left side of the room. I concentrated, trying hard to sleep again and thought about the poem I wrote for Khaye, the one where we met under the pomegranate tree, I imagined myself there. The next time I awoke it was morning. I was the first up.

Showered and dressed, I headed out. It was bright and cool. The sprinklers were watering the lawn, so I made sure I didn't get wet as I headed down the road. The buildings were identical, an ivory colour with a soft reddish tinge around the windows and tops of the doors. After glancing around I vaguely remembered the path I'd had taken in the dark early hours, and retraced my steps, walking through an archway and into a courtyard. It was so quiet I could hear the buzzing of insects and the twittering of birds, and I'm sure I heard a cock in the distance. I suddenly noticed something moving from the right and turned to look. It was a very messy grey cat, which stopped moving as soon as it noticed I was there, glaring at me suspiciously.

Khaye had a cat too, I smiled as I recalled the time she'd left her shopping out for a short while and found to her amazement the bags moving and rustling. Frightened, assuming it was a mouse, she'd frozen not knowing what to do. I couldn't believe how frightened she is of mice. Then to her relief her cat emerged as if by magic out of the bag.

I moved away from the cat and continued past the small fountain in the centre of the courtyard, watching as the feline climbed up, dipped its head forward, and sipped leisurely from the fountain. It was an adorable sight. I reached for my camera, then realised I hadn't brought it with me. Walking out of the courtyard towards the main building, I glanced back noticing that the minaret of the complex was the tallest building. Excited, and noticing that nobody was around, I turned back towards the minaret hoping I could get inside. As I approached, I saw there was no door, just an archway, so I climbed up the winding staircase. At the top, I stepped out and was captivated by the breathtaking view.

The splendour of Khaye had captivated me in the same way, but a thousand-fold. She was so generous, kind, caring and loving. It was so unfair that she had to endure torturous treatment and tremendous pain. When she'd begun experiencing the after-effects of the treatment she found it difficult to breathe and would vomit blood. I remember when her mother had once held her trying to help her in every way she could. Her father had stood frozen, the expression on his face failing to conceal his heart's aching concern and trepidation.

She looked up at him and saw the pain in his eyes and upon his face, her heart captured that moment. Her father's pain hurt her more than the treatment. She told me how I should move on, how she did not want to see me stood like that with the same pain. As tears fell on both our faces, she asked me to promise that I would take care of her books. Tasting tears on my lips, I promised I would. If only she knew I would give her my breath, my lungs, my life, my all, if I could.

I was startled by the message tone on my phone. I quickly reached for it, hoping it was her. It was my brother, checking whether I'd arrived in Spain ok. I sent a short response, as I took in the view, enjoying the mild cool breeze. There were mountains in the distance. One had a topping of white snow, and the area was very green with patches of grass and many trees. I walked around the minaret observing the same view all around; vast mountains and acres of trees. The only person to be seen was a man in the distance, tending to a field in his tractor. I stayed there basking in the view and the fresh air, absorbing the beauty of the place, the calmness, the sheer peace. I so wished she was here.

"Khaye you would so love this place," I said out loud as I thought about the lyrics of one of the last songs she'd sent me, a song by Celine Dion titled "Immortality." And I remembered, we never did say goodbye.

Cheerful Whispers

Journeys end

For many years, I wandered loves road in search
Over sand dunes and through deepest of forests
Beyond snowy mountains and most violent of volcanoes
The unlikeliest of places, we did converse

A mind more beautiful than the setting of the sun
A heart more pure than the teardrops of an angel
A voice so sweet, all animals of the world came forth to attention
A soul so much brighter, than a billion stars

Farewell to fellow travellers I did bid
I no longer wander in darkness, but now dance in the light
Upon the desert that was my heart, as rain you fell
The arid land, to bloom you did bring

I hunger for the days our eyes again meet
A smile that would tame the most ferocious of beasts
Eyes so deep that would claim the bravest of knights
On my knees, to you my heart I will gift

In exchange for my heart, your heart I will request
Cradle it in my arms and sing it lullabies I will
Wrapped in the finest of silk, bathed in the tears of angels
Take good care of your heart, I will pledge

An impregnable wall around your heart I will build
Do not fear, guarding your heart my life I will give
Your heart safe, as long as I will live

Be with it

Desire licking its lips around a freshly baked cake
Attraction to the flickering brightness of a streetlight
The need with its piercing eyes ready to pounce its prey

Oh how the burning heart in a rage is circling in its cage
Unleash this heart, this love, o master keeper of the cage
Let the love flutter around a rose so beautiful a scent so sweet

Allow it gentle nibbles on your soft delicate whispers
A few sips to quench its thirst from the wine of your eyes
Entertain it with your most enchanting melodious voice
O Like the wings of a dove, be with it, in its element in the sky

Tomorrow

Tomorrow we will dance around the trees
Tomorrow will we chase each other amid the lilies

But today my sweet let us sit and rest
Today dearest lest us take a breath

Tomorrow we will play in the pretty snow
Tomorrow will we take a walk by the steady flow

But today let us embrace and wrap up warm
Today let us by the fire tease each other until dawn

Tomorrow we will navigate the seas
Tomorrow will we fly high in the sky

But today my sweet let us explore each others eyes
Today let us gently sip our chai's

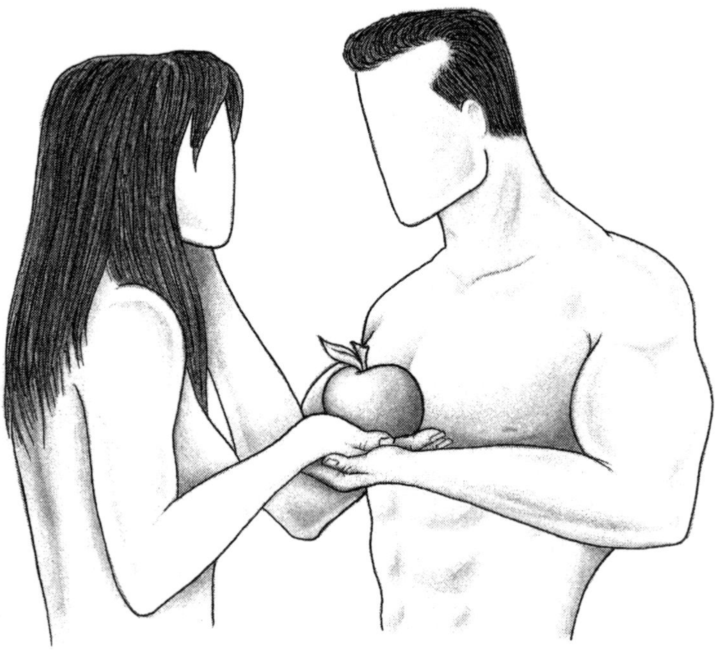

It is me

Open your eyes and recognise me
I am he who fell in love with Nefretari
He who in Cleopatra's arms died
Left desolate without Mumtaz Mahal

Look deep into my eyes can you not see me
Together we once enjoyed the apple from the tree
It was me who built you a temple at Abu Simble
With a thousand elephants built the Taj Mahal

Your soul is the soul for which mine was made
Our bond our relationship has centuries aged
We were here before and will be here again
Let us hold each other tight, until it is time, again

Sailor

Oh my love, how you did entice me
A most generous offer to sail the seas with thee
Many oceans and many seas, together we would be

Unknown it was to me, on setting sail a shore I was never to see
How taken I was with thee, gladly step aboard did me
With the sweetest of kisses, we set sail for eternity

With our hearts combined, we embraced ever so closely
Our chests dry, even in the most turbulent of seas
Your beauty, your mind, enough for me to see

Never again to touch the shore, do I want to be
Though I fear one day, you will jump and swim free
Beware my love, the earth will be flooded with tears from me
Desolate without you, this heart would be

I told her

I finally told her I did
With a heart filled with light
And courage with much might
With a large smile
I finally told her I did

She looked right
She looked left
And up at the starry night
Maybe she didn't hear me right

Again I told her I did
Her lips still closed tight
She fiddled with her tights
Ever so silent became the night
I wished I hadn't told her I did

My one and only

Many a dream of you I have seen
So long with you in love I have been
What a life together for us I have foreseen

O Seen I have the sea breeze blow your hair
Smelt I have the sweet fragrance of your air
Touched I have your skin so fair

Hand in hand we have walked many a shore
Danced we have upon the moor
O how your sweet voice I so much adore

Embraced you I have and been ever so cosy
Without you my heart would be forever lonely
My love you are my one and only

A short love letter

O Dearest I am no Burns, Shakespeare or Dunne
But since falling for you, my heart has grasped a pen
So here I sit, exercising my mind and scratching my head
To describe my love I try, but in words it cannot really be said

My sweet as a grain of sand amid the billions, as a star you sparkled
How I did find you, a miracle a marvel, I can not comprehend
From the billions and billions in this world, you it was to be
To you dearest I have gifted my all, open heartedly

O my love when you say you love me, all flowers rise and blossom
When you shower me with kisses, my heart flutters into the sky
Mountains and distances part us, but I can still reach out and touch thee
Where ever I go, ride do you my mind, sitting in my heart comfortably

Each day a memory you have gifted me, wrapped in magic and full of energy
How you always amaze me with something new from your minds library
O how the first time we did speak, for all night I did not sleep
How I questioned the wing-ed cherub "surely I am not worthy of she"

O dearest our hearts together on loves tune do always rhyme
I love you more than all the atoms, in all the universes combined
Soon I will sleep in your arms and you will awaken in mine
For I am forever only yours and you only mine

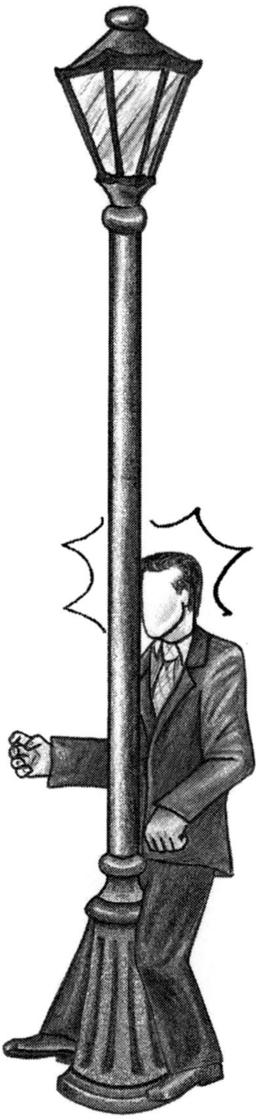

Lost

Blind as can be walking into walls is me
Lamp posts and post boxes don't escape me
Bumping into people and being cursed is me
Oh sorry, excuse me, am I saying continuously

Dribbling my soup all over my clothes is me
Knocking over food and drink repeatedly
Wearing clothes inside out now occasionally
You clown, you klutz, is every one calling me

Applying shampoo to my face am I now regularly
Rubbing moisturiser into my hair like a loony
Occasionally walking in to the road ever so blindly
The laugh of the village, am I slowly becoming to be

Asking for marijuana when I want oregano is me
Forgetting to pay for goods is so unlike me
Misplacing and losing my credit cards now frequently
Can you believe today I put salt in my tea

Oh my love what is happening to me?
I am losing track of conversations instantly
Finding myself lost in my own neighbourhood is me
Every where I look all I see is thee

You are

You are the beautiful sunrise
The early morning song bird
The whistle in the trees

You are the splendid sunset
The blossom of spring
The dance of the fairies

You are the dew upon a rose petal
The white of winter morning
The pretty moon lit seas

You are the enchanting woods
The glow of the log fire
The cool nights breeze

You are the beat of my heart
The strength in my bones
The breath in my lungs

You are my love
All my life needs

Oh how

The sea is always gently stroking the seaweed
The earth forever hugging the roots of the trees
Oh how the clouds softly play with the skies
My love, run into my arms as the rivers run into the seas

Forever do flowers open out their arms for the rays of the sun
Always do oceans kiss and stroke the face of each stone
Oh how the moon can be seen in the eyes of the sea
Dearest, touch me like a dew drop does gently touch a tree

The mountains how they reach up and touch the sky
How each wave passionately kisses the shores of the sea
Oh how the wind does gently stroke the leaves upon a tree
Sweetheart, kiss me as the scent of a rose does kiss the breeze

The beast

With a roaring rage does the beast roam the cage
Those bright piercing eyes continuously searching a glimpse
O master, keeper of the keys take pity on this beast

Look deep into his eyes let calmness posses this fiend
Unlock the cage and let this powerful beast roam free
Trust me, tamed and gentle and by your side will he always be

Comfort and affection in your arms he will seek
Starve and whither, only from your hands will he feed
Never a roar or even a squeak, gentle he will always be

Hit him, kick him and beat him, but never will he leave
In the burning heat, in the bite of the cold, by your side will he be
Where ever you will go always follow you will he

To protect his beloved, his life he will eagerly deceive
O fight to the death, to ensure no harm to his beloved will he
Be warned, it is but love that will kill this beast

Love sick

The symptoms of this sickness are complex to recognize
How the heart will pound hysterically at just the sight
The hands will tremble and voice will become stuttery
Insomnia will set in, as the mind plays her over and over again

With one touch a fever will set in, and the burning will begin
No time to spare, in the clouds you will always remain
With vision impaired, walk into lampposts you will
Damage to reasoning and thinking you will also sustain

Don't be afraid, in time some symptoms will pass
But some longer term damage, will for longer last
Be warned, regular occasions of large teary eyes
Learn you will, to live with this most powerful disease

Trust me my friend this sickness is worth the ache
A most wonderful condition for anyone to partake
Join me I say and experience this journey of bliss
Let us pray, never to be cured from this most glorious of pains

Amazing

O I like it when you lick your lips
O baby the way you twirl and tap those hips
The coyness of your eyes sends my heart into fits

The pout of your lips sends my heart a trembling
The allure of your voice sends my ears a blazing
Something amazing must be in the making

My hands are a shaking and my toes are a tingling
O baby your sweet scent sends me a hallucinating
One touch and to the heavens my soul will be a fluttering

Do

Call me write me come and meet me
Chase me hound me come and catch me
Tease me tickle me come and squeeze me
Copy me label me come and name me
Feed me cover me come and warm me
Teach me train me come and lecture me
Reign me tame me come and make me

Marry me tie me and forever bind me
Kiss me cuddle me and forever please me
Hold me hug me and forever embrace me
Ask me task me and forever assign me
Yell me bell me and forever shout me
Entertain me mime me and forever amuse me
Touch me caress me and forever adore me

Pinch me bite me but never bruise me
Mock me taunt me but never hurt me
Upset me offend me but never break me
Toss me throw me but never drop me
Fight me slap me but never leave me
Love me like me but never hate me
Bury me, cover me, but never forget me

Khaye

In each breadth, in each thought
Deep in the mind and at the back of the eyes
Carved in the heart and all over the soul

On the arms the legs, lips and the tongue
Under the skin, behind the ears even in my tears
On each strand of hair and each cell and nerve

At the ends of my toes and on the tips of my fingers
Behind my teeth and even under my nails
In the blood, on the artery's and upon each vein

Each cell with a tattoo, a marking, a stamp
Your name engraved, yours and only yours
Forever and always

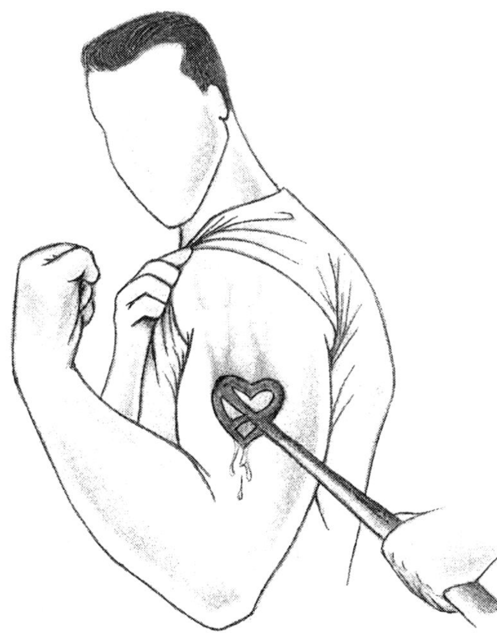

The one

The one that is unknown, lingering
Tip toeing, forever on the mind
Appearing in and out of thought
The drifter, moving from eye to eye
Dancing from dream to dream
The face in the cloud, the whistle in the trees
The lurking shadow, the whispering wind
Appearing as a quickening heart beat
Up and down side to side the shape shifter
A racing pulse even a muted voice
Suddenly gone, only to appear tiptoeing
The one that is but to conquer ones life

Proposal

A beautiful spring morning with not a soul to be seen
With my love I enjoy our regular jogging spree
This morning though I sense different from those that have been

Somewhat tired and breathless I pick a stop to breathe
Under the willow tree with my love do I take a moment to be
Looking up into the tree a eureka moment does come to me

I whisper to my love "come hither up into the tree
Sit upon this branch and carefully listen to me"
"What climb up there into the tree? Don't be so silly"

"Yes my love just the first branch, its safe trust me"
"Certainly not, have you forgotten I was once stuck up a tree"
"Trust me my darling upon the first branch sit with me"

With a hug and a gentle kiss, I help my love up the tree
After a little difficulty hand in hand, face to face is we
How her eyes sparkle in the rays of the sun so delightfully

"My love will you on this beautiful morning marry me
For you a ring fashioned from a tightly rolled leaf
With a splendid sparkling dew drop for a diamond, from me"

Tenderly stroking her cheek and pushing back her hair
In the lush gardens of her eyes an answer I seek
Waiting eagerly for her to confirm what her eyes do speak

Never forgotten

She that does pirouette on my mind
She that does dance in my heart
Never forgotten is she
With whom my soul is entwined

She that does make me smile
She that does make me all warm inside
Forever special is she
Memories of whom are so sweet and fine

Our park

On a bright day with my eyes squinting in the burning heat
I take shelter under the shade of our special tree
In the park back against the bark I sit watching the world pass

Filling bags of pollen from flower to flower is the busy bee
The leaves gently floating down from the trees
Swans stroll upon the sparkling pond as it bathes in the sun

A couple canoodling in the sun as a jogger does pass by
A mischievous child chasing a pretty squirrel up a tree
The chubbiest of blokes floating on the green sea

Above me high the pretty fairies dancing in the sky
Every now and again a breeze does hurry by
Wonder does me, will they ever name a bench after you and me

Cognitive lapse

I awoke early in the morning took a look at your portrait
I was cognitively not fully there; maybe dementia or dysphasia has set in
I said something prematurely, which came out not as I had meant it to be
My words did not match my real thoughts, and so technically not me

Ignore the words of this schizophrenic in me
I sit here on my knees hands together, pouting with difficulty
My lashes blinking immensely, I apologise profusely
Please forgive me for my lapse into stupidity
I will tighten security and ensure such a lapse never again hurts thee

In the shade of the coconut tree

In view of the rising sun and the beauty of the deep blue sea
Under the shade of the coconut tree huddled is we
The warmth of your arms the tickle of your hair pleases me
I like it when you tickle me and look up at me
Those incredible innocent eyes do make me smile

To your sweet voice and beautiful words my heart melts away
O how our hearts have embraced and now forever together play
How our souls dance to the tune of love all night and day
Though I do worry, my heart is made of the most delicate clay
My love I do appeal thee, tread gently, take care not to break me

A full moon tonight

O It's a full moon tonight
The wise one is in full flight
As the fairies gather for a fight
A shooting star does create a pretty sight
We stare at each other in the dim light

O It's a full moon tonight
As the cold does begin to bite
A sudden hoot does give us a fright
We hold each other so warm and tight
Each touch an affectionate delight

O It's a full moon tonight
The midnight creatures watch this sight
Our lips meet with passion in this twilight
As our hearts beat with so much might
We remain as one until sunlight

O my sweet, it's a full moon tonight

Intoxicated Dreamer

Regularly in my dreams, do I lie against your pomegranate tree
Your head in my lap, your eyes deep in Wuthering heights
I enjoy this dream, watching you read, as I play gently with your hair
Delicately from your forehead, each strand I move away
At times your eyes meet mine, coupled with the warmest of smiles

When not under your pomegranate tree, we travel as far as can be
As gypsies in a caravan by Blackpool tower, do we like to read
We spend our time eating pomegranates, watching the beautiful skies
Again are we at the fountain of the Alhambra, where ours lips did first meet
Hand in hand, prancing and dancing with sand beneath our feet

My heart beating, alone again with a pillow for comfort I awake
Snatched from you without a goodbye, I eagerly await for the night to fall again
As the day moves, regularly does my mind wonder, following you in the fields
These moments I enjoy, as I smile to others amusement embarrassingly
The night falls, under the covers of darkness I lie in my bed drifting
Again secretly lying under the pomegranate tree are we

I can see

Oh so much beauty I did see
The prettiest of flowers, the beauty of trees
The rising tide the setting sun
The splendour of so many living things

For many years on the search for true love was me
Flower to flower searching for the flawless rose would I be
The perfect love I did seek but imperfections always a familiarity
Darkness fell, never love I did think I would see

Wondering in the darkness a scent did draw me
With deep breaths following my nose did I meet thee
A voice so beautiful I mistook for a sweet melody
Your laugh an injection of ecstasy

Your melodious voice did encapsulate me
Your heart of such purity, floating in the clouds was me
In the darkness I just wanted to dance with glee
Always taking deep breaths of your scent was me

Your smile projected clearly in my mind for all the cells to see
Your eyes your lips an oil painting hung in my minds library
For your sweet melodies, oh ache did me
Can it be that I have fallen in love with thee

How can one love when one can not see, you question me
Dearest, I may be blind and not see physically
But trust me I see more clearly than all those that can see
A blind mans love is the most potent than there can be
My love, my feelings are true for thee

We

Across the candle eyes entwined
Sharing sweet words twisting her hair
Minds together in a world far away
Gentle touching hands across the way

Hand in hand in the glow of the lamp
Under the full moon walking in the sand
Sharing affectionate glances coupled with a smile
Watching the ocean kiss the shore time after time

Fingers softly combing each others hair
The warmest of breaths then a passionate kiss
Breast meets breast and tongues are entwined
Lost in each others arms for the end of time

Exploring each other under the cover of darkness
Making love in the glow of the horizon
Gently retreating and returning with the ocean
In tandem "I love you" again and again softly spoken

My flower lady

The roses the lilies and the pretty poppies
The sofa my armchair lost amongst the posies
Buttercups tulips and even pink freesias
Where did my lady regularly acquire such beauties?

An old man in the café with difficulty did he drink his tea
Without hesitation my lady pulled out her stethoscope to help he
Referring him to hospital, how seriously ill was he
"Oh thank you kind lady, may god bless thee"
Daffodils roses and even pink posies arrived all day for she

An autistic boy, experiencing discrimination continuously
To my lady, his mother pleaded, please help he
Justice and funding did my superb lady acquire for he
"Oh wonderful women, how can we thank thee?"
A large bouquet of flowers, the prettiest of delicate lilies for she

As proud as can be always tripping over flowers is me
My newspaper and books missing amongst the posies
The scent of the narcissus always wrapped around me
Surrounded by flowers, but the most beautiful of all is she

Precious gift

The most delicate, flawless, smoothest and softest of silk he did use
The rarest and beautiful pair of emeralds he did choose
The finest gold, spun by the most experienced of angels he did use

Carefully did he construct the mind, each cell individually assessed
The heart moulded from feathers of an angel and in the oceans of heaven blessed
A body sculptured by a master to whom Michelangelo cannot compare his best

Under the pretty glow of dawn, thirty days today, did he gift she
A most precious gift from him, to this unworthy earth and we
One can only imagine, how he did manage to part from she

As she wonders through the fields, the flowers stand in attention
Time stands still, all creatures stop and sit up to watch in concentration
All marvel the most alluring of auras, the most amazing intoxication

In my dreams she first embraced me and from my thoughts never apart
Her compassion and sweet voice did polish loves poisonous dart
How with better aim than Paris did she pierce my heart

Like a phoenix from the ashes I arose, love burning with an eternal blaze
As she entered my life I came alive, my future fell into place
She touched my heart which spread its wings and flew into space

What can a mere me offer she, on this most unique day of her anniversary
Wrapped delicately my heart, body and soul I have already gifted to she
As I write it does come to me, I have but one gift left to offer she and only she
My beloved, forever and always, in my poetry immortalised will she be

For as long

For as long as the sun does burn
The stars retain their shine
And the galaxies grow and expand
My heart, your love will always command

For as long as the clouds roam the skies
The sun slowly sinks into the sea
And the moon lights up the dark night
Your image in my eyes will remain so bright

For as long as a dove spreads its wings
Eagles fly high above in the sky
And marmosets on the trees rely
My beloved for you I will never shy

For as long as roses do blossom
The scent of the narcissus does mix with the sky
And leaves gently float in the autumn
In my dreams my love you will always be welcome

Wedding vow

My love forever and always to you my heart I bind
To be open and share with you all that is mine
Forever keep my eyes for you and to all others be blind

Never to be afraid if you speak from your heart openly
If you are ever unhappy to hold you and kiss you gently
Never to raise my voice and to only ever speak softly

To comfort you and never let your heart pine
Hold you close and in my arms keep you enshrined
To always support you in all that you do and help you shine

If you're ever hurt or upset to tickle you and hug you tightly
With actions show you I love you morning noon and nightly
To always love and care for you even when you get old and wrinkly

Catch any tears wipe away any fears and ensure you're happy
Stand tall in the face of challengers that may face we
My love with this ring I bind we, like the earth to the roots of a tree

Day away

Darling again, off to work is me
Being away from thee is such a difficulty
Counting the minutes until lunchtime will I be
At noon hurry to the phone to enjoy your voice will me

Sat at my desk always thinking of thee
Dancing on clouds, lying in the fields I appear to be
Under the sun, under the stars do I disappear off with thee
Always wishing you were here with me

Walking hand in hand, enjoying the park I see we
Lying in bed playing with each others hair I dream are we
Far away from each other, yet so close to thee is me
My love I am forever dreaming of thee
Oh when will work end, so I can be home with thee

Without a word

Walking the lonely road ever so quietly
How she crept up and hit me ever so sweetly
O fellow travellers can you believe what she did to me

Without a word, without asking me
She took my heart and escaped
Without a whisper, without a word
She took my heart and ran away

Dazed and confused without a fight
In her beauty did I let her take advantage of me
O listen, it was the prettiest of faces I did ever see

Without a word, without asking me
She took my heart and escaped
Without a whisper, without a word
She took my heart and ran away

On my knees in the cold and palpitating
Lost and unable to find my way home she left me
O creatures of the night, gather round and hear my story

Without a word, without asking me
She took my heart and escaped
Without a whisper, without a word
She took my heart and ran away

This mind and soul now this lady's to keep
The one I have dreamt about on this lonely road is she
O people hear me, blinded I am and need her light to guide me

Without a word, without asking me
She took my heart and escaped
Without a whisper, without a word
She took my heart and ran away

Sat in the cold wilderness am I awaiting she
My pretty lady hurry back and with you take me
O fellow travellers, she is the one to walk the aisle with me

No more sharing

O the warmth of the sun is finally arriving
The clouds have had their day and now dispersing
With them they will take all your days of aching
And soon a new day for us will be dawning

O listen brighter days will be on their way soon
The end is near for this terrible typhoon
No longer will there be a regular monsoon
You will again endure and forever leave this cocoon

O let the warmth of happiness again take hold
Awaken your spirit and bring it in from the cold
Let us begin again our story and let the magic unfold
Loudly let it be spoken that is yet to be told

O how bright and beautifully the sun will shine
No longer watching your pain will this heart pine
No more sharing, again you will just be mine
It has been a long time coming, but now all will be fine

My sweet maid

Take heed sweet maiden my heart is tough soil
To work it will take much effort and toil
Heavily trodden having endured years of draught
Difficult it is to get ought to sprout

With a will so strong plough she did
Delicate hands reached deep in the dirt
Digging and digging turning the soil
With love and care how gently she sowed

With her tears and sweat softening the soil
The clouds observing did begin to wail
Who would have thought green shoots would spring
As time is passing a lush garden is growing

Beautiful narcissus and an unimaginable scent
Trees and shrubbery below a pretty blue heaven
Now apples, grapes and large plump pears
Oh how I owe all to my sweet maid

For only thee

My sweet, there is a heart that beats
A soul that always beckons
And a mind always wrapped in thee

My darling, there are eyes that thirst
A skin that yearns
And ears always perked up for thee

My love, an embrace always awaiting
Every atom screaming
And lips parched without thee
Oh come and take advantage of me

My secret

Under the cover of darkness, watched by the sparkling stars
With ease I search my mind, as always your voice I find
Remembering how, I would be lost in the depths of your eyes

My heart starts swelling, as your record begins playing
The silent thoughts, slowly start singing and dancing
Hand in hand, gently floating high into the misty skies

Oh my love, if only you knew about the secret I do hide
The truth of how much I love you, I keep locked in my mind
My love of such magnitude, afraid I am to let loose into the wild

The world would end, such love it cannot comprehend
Remember this beloved, if ever we are forced apart
Forever will you remain, in the depths of this heart of mine

Echo

As I lie in bed in the depths of thought
All alone and without your warmth
The echoes of my heart rise as pretty colours
Caught by the air and carried by the wind
Gently taken floating in the heavens
From molecule to molecule drifting
Come upon your willow to rest upon a leaf
Gently carried through your window
Resting upon your bed as you lie sleeping

Tearful Whispers

Lovers parted

I am the tears of the long departed
The voice of the broken hearted
The pain of those lovers parted

How we were the envy of the lonely
Hated by those in a bond of misery
Loathed by those with all but love aplenty

How we were loves epitome
Our scent desired by many a wasp and bee
Rivalled Mozart did our loves symphony

How we were the aspiration for many
Jealousy of the pilgrims still on their journey
A writers inspiration for many a story

How we were subject to inevitability
How we were gullible to life's predictability
To suffer the fate of many before we

I am the tears of the long departed
The voice of the broken hearted
The pain of those lovers parted

The last goodbye

The evening is cold, the evening is wet
Your arms are warm, your words comforting
Darkness is near, though I feel no fear
Your touch is tender, your lips so sweet
You tighten your hold, as mine falters

The clock is ticking, darkness is falling
Your tears are warm, the embrace comforting
My lips betray me, but my eyes speak silently
The ticking is stopping, my eyes reveal a smile
Forever and always, in your eyes, stay mine

Beside my love

Birds twittering, sun shining
Joyful skipping, heart dancing
Flowers blooming my love smiling

Sudden bang crash heart jumping
Unbearable thoughts mind racing
Broken bones my love bleeding

Running falling begging and pleading
Seeking and staggering heart pounding
Tears falling my love not breathing

Rushing feet numerous voices
Loud sirens and flashing lights
Pumping breathing my love moving

Machines contraptions constant bleeping
Tubes bags and auto feeding
A delicate touch my love groaning

Passing days, sleepless nights
Tears, quivering lips and silent words
Hand in hand my love improving

A gentle kiss, a warm embrace
No more tears and a smiling face
Heart in hand, beside my love always

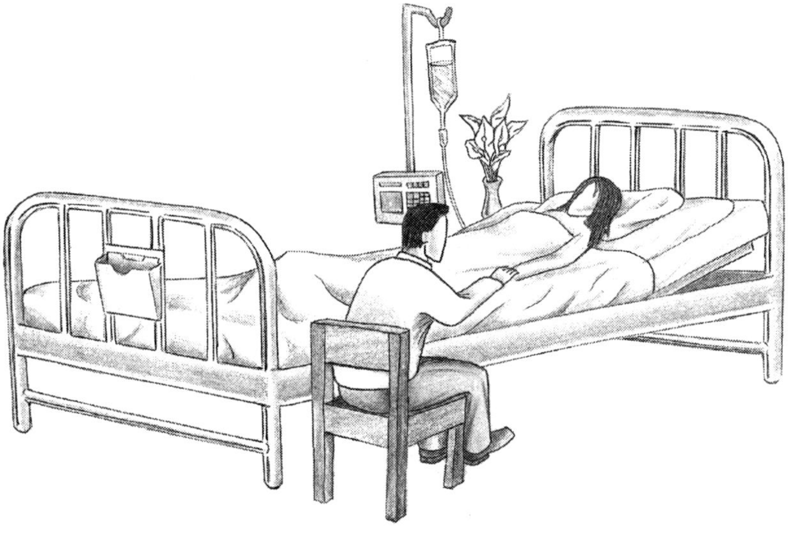

Cuffed

Swimming in thy tranquil eyes and floating in thy voice
Intoxicated with thy love, cupid did cuff me to thee
Joined until the end of time, never parted can we be
Mind, heart and soul entwined for eternity

Intoxicated on love, a cursed disease has taken advantage of we
I am sorry my love for failing to protect thee
This cursed illness is much more powerful than mere me
But believe me, my love is potent, in time I will attract its attention to me

Remember in thy dreams it is me who always leave's thee
This coincides with the dream that I reported in my early poetry
Remember it is me, who will in thy arms go ever so quietly
He may remove me, but my heart and soul will stay with thee

My love trust me, an old lady along time ago did say to me
"Thou will love a fair golden haired lady, who a difficult time will see
But don't worry my child, a recovery and a little girl I do see
Forever in happiness together will thee be"

So believe me, again running in the park like Christie will thee
Singing and dancing and playing the violin for me
Full of energy travelling the world together we will be
So painful it is, but please take thy medication and chemo therapy

"My love, if thou loves me move on", thee do say to me
"My love, find a new love and forget about me"
How selfless is thee, but these words do hurt me
My love understand there is no key to the cuffs that bind we

Sweetheart, remember cuffed is me, so always with thee
So please don't ignore me and speak to me
Reminding me to chew my food and eat slowly
Copy my accent, joke and tease me

My love, thy silence is much too painful for me
Unable to eat or sleep, fed from thy hands does me want to be
Where ever thy go I will follow in every eventuality
I love thee and thy loves me, so let us together be
Darling, embrace me and like the Nile let my love flow free
For I am for eternity, cuffed to thee

Awaiting the day

How ever long it takes no matter how far you are
In the snow in the rain come thunder and hail
In the light of day in the dark of night
To be with you forever, I am awaiting the day

Remembering your laugh and taste of your tears
Your silky soft skin and smell of your hair
The intoxicating eyes and energetic ways
Steadfast and awake, I am awaiting the day

Alone now watching the autumn leaves fall
Blooming of flowers, oh the beauty of spring
Warmth of the summer and the chill of the winter
Not now the same, for you I am awaiting the day

Remembering our cooking and food fighting those days
Oh how I liked putting ice-cream on your face
Running around the kitchen like school children was our play
Can't be done alone, for you I am awaiting the day

Remembering running in the countryside in wellies with you
Pleasure at theatre shows plays and concerts too
Long drives picturesque places not the same without you
Here forever and always waiting, awaiting the day
Awaiting the day, to be with you

Never alone

Thoughts and memories sitting as one
Listening to the wind and the moving leaves
Embraced they watch the sunset and rise
Oh how they enjoy counting the stars

Feeding each other grapes sat by the Rhine
Intoxicating each other on loves vintage wine
Whispering sweet nothings in each other ears
Oh how with so much strength I hold back the tears

Never any end to their joyful manner
Oh how they dance around the still burning fire
Teasing and joking tickling and laughing
How so full of energy never do they tire

Chasing each other into the once lush fields
Embracing and kissing in the shade of our willow
Playing and singing all night and day
How fortunate never ever parted are they

The house they have taken where you once lived
My heart they make their permanent base
Together forever until time does end
Oh how never alone is a heart that has loved and bled

One midsummer's day

My heart was chained, held in a cage in a land far away
Feelings and emotions all locked away
Carefully guarded for the one to take away

One mid summer's day the sweetest voice did come my way
Like a candle, did the chains melt and fall away
Feelings and emotions, came out to play

Days of joyful playing were on their way
Smiling, joking and dancing was now my way
With happiness and great pleasure, lovers game I did play

Carefully wrapped in silk, my heart I did give away
Intoxicated and in the clouds I was away
New words, I love you, I would say

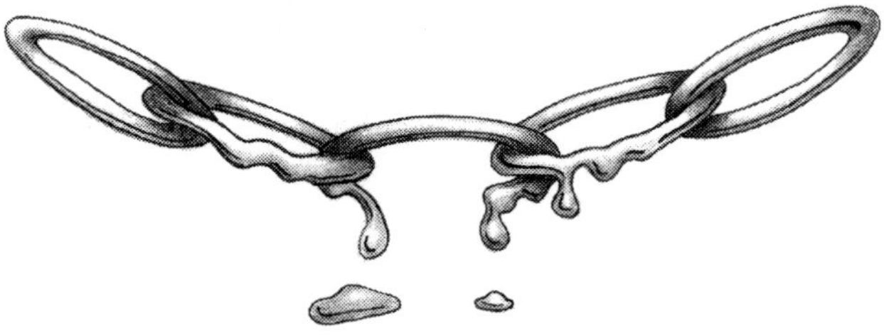

My mind with ideas of marriage, it did play
Excited and sure, marry me I did say
Sharing my life was now the only way

Happy and jubilant I was dancing away
When one dark day a tragedy did come my way
Much pain and sorrow, was on its way

God stop this unfairness, I did say
Tears day and night were now on their way
Only with memories and thoughts was I now to play

Alone and upset, in the park I now spend many a day
Listening to heart-rending music now my way
The world has no importance, do I now say

Oh how her sweet scent still blows me away
But happiness and laughter no longer my way
The pain is unbearable, please take it away
To be with her for eternity, I do pray

Why does it feel so real?

Every night she touches my face ever so gently
Looks deep into my eyes, with so much love
Slowly, running her fingers through my hair adoringly

With her head against my chest, she holds me tightly
Slowly and tenderly, does she kiss my lips
In her hands, she cups my face and whispers so softly

"Wake up my love it's a new day, wake up my love it's a new day"
I listen to her sweet symphony and open my eyes
To my disappointment find, she did not stay, she did not stay

Awaiting thee

Awaiting and awaiting thee
My breath has begun to break free
Come quickly and embrace me
For one last time touch me

My eyes soon will no longer see
Come quickly before they close for eternity
Enter these eyes, once more let them see thee
Hurry the sun is setting, I will soon be free

I must travel all alone and without thee
O my love, do not let me depart
Without one more time whispering
How much I love thee
Hurry I am awaiting thee, awaiting thee

On my way

The pain the tears now unbearable for me
Sleepless nights and the loss of appetite
No longer can I fight my longing for thee

With my bags packed on my way is me
My body and soul like magnets drawn to thee
I love thee, thy loves me, together forever we will be

Dreaming of thy smile and melodious voice
Imagining thy warmth embrace and intoxicating eyes
My love, thy open arms I do see awaiting me

Hungary and thirsty my beloved I will be
With a delicate kiss, quench my thirst
With thy sweet hands, please feed me

Over the hills and down the winding roads
Along the Roman road and up the village lane
My love a compass, thy heart my guide
Sweetheart, on my way is me

Why not me?

A beautiful mind, with the most caring heart
Compassionate, loving and the most forgiving
Selfless, trusting and the most understanding
Why her with all this unbearable suffering?

Splendid dimples and the most beautiful smile
Fair soft skin and rosy pink cheeks
Innocent eyes and the voice of an angel
Why her in misery and unable to sit at the table?

Green fingers and a love for Mother Nature
A passion for learning and so much teaching
For the disadvantaged, her time spent caring
Why her, with such difficulty breathing?

The most fantastic of cooks, what splendid curries
Heavenly Shepard's pie, lets not forget her Ras Malai
What marvellous desserts, her carrot cake such a delight
Why her, now unable to devour or taste even a slice?

Full of energy, running swimming and even rock climbing
A love for skiing, lacrosse and even belly dancing
Ballet, salsa and even ballroom for this dancing queen
Why her all drowsy pumped up on morphine?

In pain, with fear and doubts, she remains the most caring
Smiling she still teases me, funny nicknames she creates for me
My accent she still likes, my intrusive schwa she loves
Why her, why not me, why not me?

Foreseen

You came into my life like a gust of wind
Tickling my ears and ruffling up my feathers
With you, you did bring much hope and joy
A life I could see full of love, comfort and ecstasy

I see you sat at a grand piano playing fine tunes
Children sitting and singing to your sweet melodies
You helping the elderly, the sick and all those in need
How my intrusive schwa, you do like indeed

At the fountain of Alhambra, on my knees I propose to thee
Henna so beautiful on the fairest of hands I do see
In an ivory wedding dress you look so pretty
Clumsily you lose your duppata during the evening activity

I see us enjoying the sights of Russia, China and Peru
Plays, concerts and romantic theatre shows too
Days at antique's fairs, museums and art galleries
Many days in Blackpool, living like gypsies

Gardening and planting I do see us enjoy
Throwing flour and tickling each other in the kitchen a joy
In the study reading, writing and sharing glances at each other are we
In the bedroom dancing bouncing all night long, would we be

Our favourite place the library, endless hours spend there would we
Places where we could gain knowledge we like to be
Evenings dancing the salsa and jiving I do see
Lying by a warm open fire enjoying each others company are we

Competing in cooking dinners for friends and relatives I see
Your cousins flexing their muscles in the conservatory
Gramps asleep in the hammock snoring so loudly
You I see, trying to help a bird and getting stuck up in a tree

Me taking lessons from your father in photography
Together, going for week long drives in the countryside I see
In the heights of happiness and the depths of sadness
Together guiding each other through the jungle are we

Our children I see, the brightest that can be
Pretty little Elisa, her copy of the independent she does enjoy
Alam what a cute boy, a violin his favourite toy
Many languages do we teach them, their education a priority

This cursed disease I did not see, together we can overcome it, believe me
Growing old and wrinkly together I do foresee
My love you will get better and we can make it all a reality

Prettiest Pear

Sitting in the shade of the prettiest pear tree
Up in the branches high, something caught my eye
The brightest green pear enjoying the sun carefree
Did the pickers not see this splendour, high in the sky?
Had it been too wonderful, or just out of reach
Or maybe it had eluded the pickers awaiting me
Hiding until the pickers had picked enough each
Convinced it was destiny, I climbed deep into the tree
My fear of heights vanished without even a sign
Up high, I climbed and climbed, my eyes fixed to the prize
The green sparkle in my eyes, this pear almost mine
A sudden slip and a dance away went my stance
Into the distance, vanish did the pear from my eyes
How unfairly short lived was this remarkable romance

A little wiser

Under the rays of the burning sun
Strolling through the park having fun
Across an amazing creature of Eden I did come

Intoxicated by those bright green eyes
Mesmerised by those fair slender thighs
Reach out I did though it was unwise

Bite me she did and disappear into the misty skies
In pain and bleeding no one could hear my silent cries
Wondering through the park blind, now am I a little wise

The bed

As she lay in bed
How many times
Had she coughed and bled
Over the side
Thrown up and cried
How many nights
Had she dreamt and wept
To get up
Had she stumbled and fell
To even hold me
Has she been weak and frail
O lord please put wind in her sail
Let her no longer be pale
Free her from this jail

Immortal is me

I am the warmth of the sun
On thy skin embracing thee
I am the whispering wind
In the trees forever calling thee
I am the air all around
Always watching over thee

I am the leaves from our tree
That gently fall and kiss thee
I am the cold raindrops
That playfully tickle thee
I am the early morning hum
That gently awakens thee

I am thy comfy pillow
That in the night comforts thee
I am the warm soapy water
That gently bathes thee
I am thy silent shadow
Forever standing by thee

I am a thought I am a memory
The most beautiful vivid dream
My love I am forever here
Don't shed a tear for me
I am forever only thine
Never gone, immortal is me

Cut from the rose

Darkness is falling as the clouds are hopelessly wandering
For one is the boat at the shore ready for sailing
Parting hands with finger tips trying hard to remain touching
Eyes fixed to the beloved slowly into the distance disappearing

Cut is the stem from the rose and left aching
With tears falling and the heart palpitating
Cut is the stem from the rose and left forever perishing

A grey mist upon the land slowly begins creeping
As a mighty earthquake does hit the heart sending it shaking
The lush gardens and pretty meadows all but diminishing
Fields of lilies, poppies and roses bowed down grieving

Cut is the stem from the rose and left aching
With tears falling and the heart palpitating
Cut is the stem from the rose and left forever perishing

The warmth and comfort of the sun now fading
Oh what a terrible punishment for a lover to be receiving
With the power of an atom bomb is each tear falling
With much difficulty does the lover keep breathing

Cut is the stem from the rose and left aching
With tears falling and the heart palpitating
Cut is the stem from the rose and left forever perishing

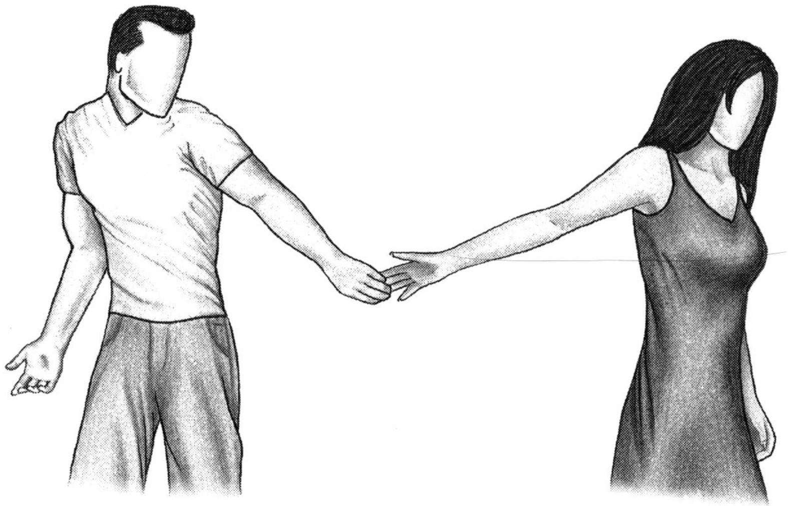

Fear mere me

Mere me as David will Goliath slay
As Samson bring down the citadel around he
Raise the army of Alexander and triumph will me

With the power of Hercules will I wrestle he
With cunning, the power of Medusa attain will me
Turn to stone on approach will he

An army of armed winged cherubs will aid me
Souls of lovers past will form a wall around thee
My love never near thee, will I allow he

Hide thee in the lighthouse of Pharos will me
The Golden Fleece I will acquire for thee
My love, I will do all in my power to protect thee

Make him an offer he can't refuse will me
Track him to the ends of the earth and beyond will me
Let him fear the power of love, within mere me

The calling

Across the turbulent seas
Sat amongst the wild roses
Her eyes are but seeking me

Dancing under the Gulmohar tree
Pretty red leaves falling around she
Each twirl but a message to me

Sat at the table of our forefathers
Eating grapes and sipping tea
Her mind but only focused on me

Playing her grandmothers violin
With such passion and feeling
The depth of each tune calling for me

O lord my calling has come, now let me be
Now let me be

Left behind

An impression left on the stone by the tide
The tide long gone no longer can the stone confide

How the land has been left barren and empty
Completely naked and bare like an autumn tree

The heart grounded like a dove without wings and never free
Forever and always locked in a cage without a key

Dreams as delicate raindrops have fallen away
But thoughts and memories still tickle the brain and stay

One day the sun will set and the wind will no longer blow this way
The air will stop breezing and the pain will slowly fade away

Fair swap

Dearest my smiles and laughter, are yours to keep
My sweet dreams, to have in your sleep
My strength and stamina, for you for keeps

Swap me the wheezing and difficult nights sleeping
Runs in the park, with difficulty breathing
All the fainting, coughing and bleeding

My love your smiles and joyful dancing, you gifted me
It is time to exchange, it's my turn for all this misery
A fair swap my dearest, please believe me

Prayer

With my hands together and on my knees
O god I do ask thee please let her be
To my heart please do not cause any more injury

I ask thee take my life and give it to she
Her pain and tears give them to me
I volunteer eagerly please hear me

I pray thee do not part me from she
She is me as me is she
Our souls are one and together we must be
If you must, together I pray thee take we

Gone

The night was humid, the night was long
No more sleeping, now that she is gone
My eyes all red and puffy from all the tears that have ran

The lush garden of my heart, unattended and dieing
The smell of Narcissus now into the sky, gently fading
The charm of her voice, preserved in my thinking

My energy and my will now all but spent
My smiles and laughter, with her I sent
Without a heart, mind and soul, unable to survive
A one way ticket to her I will find

Elephant driver

On the lush banks of the river Nile
Beside the mighty Borasus palms
The wise old elephant driver fore told me
A pair of absinthe eyes, are in your destiny

Whilst walking the lonely road carefree
A bolt of lightning fulfilled this prophecy
The deepest emerald eyes, possessed me
Under my spell, were now wealth and prosperity

The relationship flawless and most sublime
Hearts together to the same tune did rhyme
Enjoyment and splendour all without time
Night and day intoxicated, on the most splendid wine

Asleep in each others arms unaware of the dark cloud
It surrounded the room, turning all upside down
Out of my arms, viciously seized was my crown
Carried off into the sky, as the sun came down

Cold and hungry, no more wine, no more joyful play
All alone and in pain, to be with my crown I pray
Everything grey, frozen, looking like Pompeii
Little about these days, does the elephant driver ever say

Beloved's road

Unnoticed lying somewhere out in the cold
With an incomplete soul have i been growing old
Regularly do i retrace our steps on our road of old
Where your scent still wonders like untarnished gold
How In the playful breeze, your voice still echoes

Unfinished, our story has been left to remain untold
Though my mind plays all those dreams that didn't unfold
My arms ache with the want to have you again to hold
Soon my love it will be my turn to walk your road
Again in my eyes and my arms, i will hold you close

Listen

Listen to me sweetheart
Hear the voice of this heart
And the words of these eyes

Return, for I will greet thee with pearls
Manufactured in mine eyes
Come, I will greet thee with warmth
From the tamed fire of mine heart

Listen to me sweetheart
Hear the talk of this mind
Return my love and again be mine

Melancholy

Wear does the face a smile all but dried
Sorrow now around the mind in a tightly knot tied
Eyes always and forever remaining in full tide
The heart with so much difficulty the pain does hide

Only in an empty room is the heart set free
The tear ducts await and eagerly use this opportunity
Forming a puddle from which she looks up at me
With a raised eye brow does she end, this melancholy

One more whisper

The atria and ventricles apart
Without a rhythm is the beating of the heart

The body does pound for the beloveds touch,
Yearning for an embrace or even a kiss

The eyes constantly seeking for just one moment
To fill up on smiles and pretty emotions

The ears parched for the sweetest melody
The lips trembling to be touched

Like a starving child with hands out stretched
The heart, one more whisper does request

CPSIA information can be obtained at www.ICGtesting.com
Printed in the USA
BVOW011242160312

285364BV00001B/299/P

9 781468 157291